D0315820

BURNING UP

BURNING UP

ON TOUR WITH THE JONAS BROTHERS

By Joe, Kevin & Nick Jonas

WITH **LAURA MORTON**

PHOTOGRAPHY BY **ROB HOFFMAN**

PUFFIN

PUFFIN BOOKS

Published by the Penguin Group
Penguin Books Ltd, 80 Strand, London WC2R 0RL, England
Penguin Group (USA) Inc., 375 Hudson Street, New York, New York 10014, USA
Penguin Group (Canada), 90 Eglinton Avenue East, Suite 700, Toronto, Ontario, Canada M4P 2Y3
(a division of Pearson Penguin Canada Inc.)
Penguin Ireland, 25 St Stephen's Green, Dublin 2, Ireland (a division of Penguin Books Ltd)
Penguin Group (Australia), 250 Camberwell Road, Camberwell, Victoria 3124, Australia
(a division of Pearson Australia Group Pty Ltd)
Penguin Books India Pvt Ltd, 11 Community Centre, Panchsheel Park, New Delhi – 110 017, India
Penguin Group (NZ), 67 Apollo Drive, Rosedale, North Shore 0632, New Zealand
(a division of Pearson New Zealand Ltd)
Penguin Books (South Africa) (Pty) Ltd, 24 Sturdee Avenue, Rosebank, Johannesburg 2196, South Africa

Penguin Books Ltd, Registered Offices: 80 Strand, London WC2R 0RL, England

puffinbooks.com

First published in the USA by Disney Hyperion Books, an imprint of Disney Book Group 2008
Published in Great Britain in Puffin Books 2009
1

Designed by Stuart Smith

British Library Cataloguing in Publication Data
A CIP catalogue record for this book is available from the British Library

ISBN: 978–0–141–32685–6

Jonas Enterprises

Contents

This is Nick Jon
making a differen
together with kid
to live strong
on your dre
Your mu
Thanks for
find the
reach in
love,

Introduction

Hey, everyone, thank you so much for checking out our book. It's such an honour for us. We are thrilled to share this rare and never-before-seen collection of photos that depict our favourite memories of being on the road. We always try to keep you in the loop on what's happening with us by regularly posting on our blog and putting up new videos on YouTube that we make just for you. With this book we want to open up our lives in a special way so that you can experience the excitement and fun we get to live each and every day.

Much like our 'When You Look Me in the Eyes' video, where we show you what it's like being on the road, this book is our way of revealing our most unforgettable and intimate moments both on stage and off. You can see the joy we feel every time we get to see our fans and why we do what we do. We didn't want you to miss out on a single adventure – and the crazy roller-coaster ride we've been on!

Things really started taking off for us in February 2007, when we signed with Hollywood Records. We released our self-titled album in the USA that August, and in its first week of release, the album went to the number five slot on the Billboard Hot 200 chart. We were psyched for our future and we had assembled the right team to work with who had faith in us and who saw the same potential we saw in ourselves. We had found the perfect home with Hollywood Records and the ride was just beginning.

This book is the compilation of the next year and a half of our lives, including the Best of Both Worlds tour, where we opened for our good friend Miley Cyrus, and our first headlining tour, Look Me in the Eyes, with lots of fun and unforgettable stops in between. Plus there are photos of us recording our album, *A Little Bit Longer*, along with preparations for our Burning Up tour, where we stopped at 43 cities across the US. We hope you'll enjoy this behind-the-scenes look at life on and off the road with us, our family, our crew, and everyone who helped get us to where we are today – most especially you, our fans. You'll see that we're really a lot like you. We're not an 'act', we're just three brothers from New Jersey who are living our dream.

We love music, touring and travelling. But most of all, we wake up every day thinking about how much we appreciate the dedication of our fans. Without you, we'd be nowhere. We couldn't ask for anything more than the love, support and joy each of you gives us. It's impossible to put into words how much you all mean to us. So instead, we'll just keep rockin' to let you all know that we're thankful for every moment!

We love you,
Kevin, Joe and Nick

Hello, We're the Jonas Brothers

We'd like to take this opportunity to properly introduce ourselves. There's a lot more to the three of us than just our 'onstage' personas. We thought it would be fun to share a little bit about us offstage too. Even though people like to point out the differences between us, there are quite a few similarities, like our passion for music and our strong ties to our family and friends. Those are the most important things to all of us.

KEVIN

Hi. My name is Kevin Jonas II, and I was born on 5 November 1987. I play the lead guitar and sing. I am the oldest brother, and I love what I do.

People think of me as the businessman of the group. I really pay attention to what goes on during a tour. I enjoy being a part of the day-to-day decision-making on the road as well as off. I can easily see myself transitioning into producing or managing other artists someday. I'd love to have my own record label, discover and develop new talent, and give them the same opportunity Hollywood Records has given to us.

My Guitar Collection

One of my passions in life is collecting guitars. The guitar has become my escape no matter what's happening in my life. I always feel safe when I play.

I own around fifteen or sixteen guitars. Some of them come on the road with me, while others stay at home. But I really miss the ones I don't bring on tour. One of the first things I do when I get home is pull a few of my favourites out and play them.

My first guitar was a 1969 Gibson Les Paul Gold Top. Once I played that guitar, I knew I had to have it. Even so, my all-time favourite is my white Gibson Les Paul Supreme with gold hardware. I totally freaked out when I first saw it. These days, that one is my baby. I'm a Les Paul guy – it's just who I am. There's something about the tone, feel and heaviness of the body that completely gets to me. It just feels right.

Doing one of my guitar spins. I can get going pretty fast. It sometimes freaks people out that I can spin like that and play the guitar. It takes practice, but I love doing it.

Left: Onstage with my guitar, it's easy to get caught up in the moment.

Right: I am playing an acoustic guitar in this song, which is so different from rocking on one of my electric guitars. I really feel inspired from being up onstage. My smile says it all!

Opposite page: Jumping off one of the risers during our show in Nashville while playing 'S.O.S.' I remember that day because I got so much air coming off the ramp – a lot more than I usually do. That was, by far, the highest I jumped that entire tour. The audience was shocked at how high I flew. I have to admit, so was I. Even though I almost fell off the stage, the exhilarating feeling I got midair was definitely worth it!

Style

Our stylist, Michelle Tomaszewski, works with us to help create our individual looks. She gets that we each have our own style and preferences and helps to pull together items that carry out that image. Our current wardrobe favourites consist mainly of ties, waistcoats, ascots and really nice shoes. What's fun is that we pretty much wear the same clothes on and off stage. We don't wear ties because we have to – we genuinely like to.

Left: Michelle T., our awesome stylist

Musical Influences

There are so many artists whom I respect and admire, including Elvis Costello, Johnny Cash, Stevie Wonder, Keith Urban and Garth Brooks. Country music might seem like an unlikely influence, but I have a tremendous appreciation for the storytelling aspect, which we strive to achieve in our own songwriting.

I've listened to John Mayer for years. He is one of my favourite performers. His songwriting has greatly influenced my own. I really got into playing the guitar because his songs are such an inspiration.

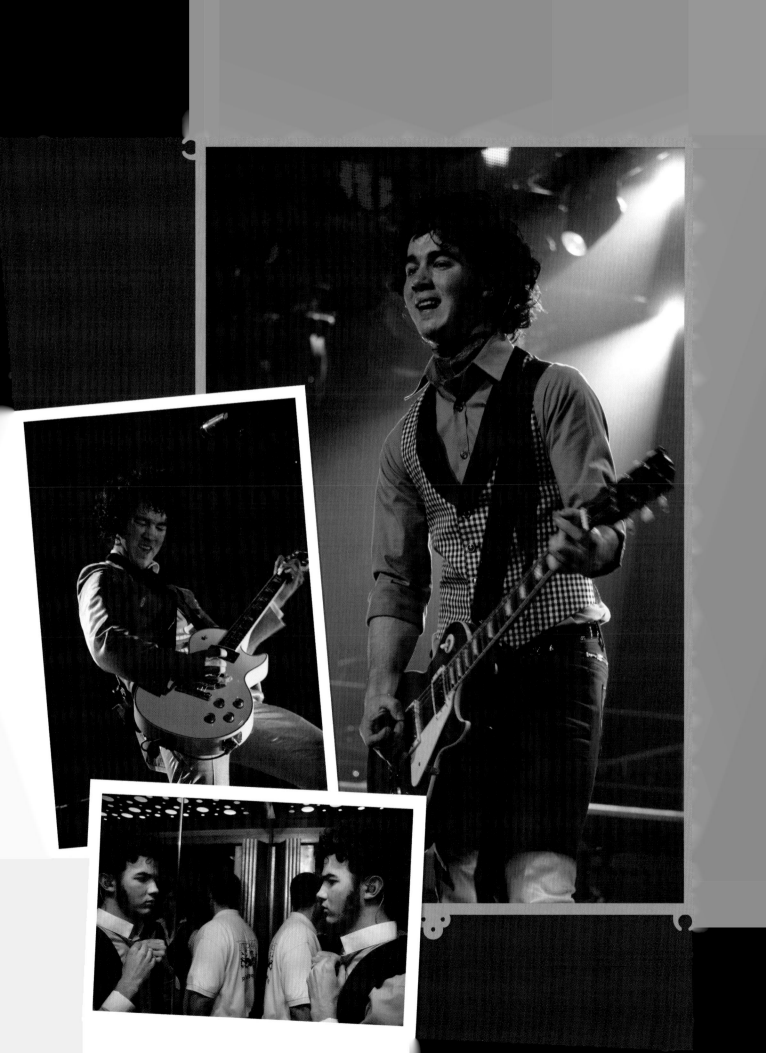

Moments of Peace

While on our recent European tour, I got to walk around Barcelona late at night. There were absolutely no people on the streets. I could just be by myself and walk around without a care in the world and no place to be. I love touring a new city I've never been in before, taking in the sites and the local scene. It's especially nice when I can go somewhere and just be another tourist. It's the best feeling ever, and one I wouldn't change. Those are rare moments, but I look forward to having them whenever possible. They're truly the ones I'll remember forever.

My Favourite Things

Favourite ice cream:
Rocky road

Favourite movie:
About a Boy

Favourite sport:
Golf

Definition of joy:
Something you can't express or put into words, but it feels really good and makes you happy

If I weren't a pop star, I'd like to be:
An astronaut

Most influential person in my life:
My father

I collect:
Gibson Les Paul guitars

Best advice someone gave me:
'Watch the mistakes of the people you admire the most and don't make those same mistakes.'

Favourite gadget:
My BlackBerry

I can't live without:
Cell phone service

Best part of being on the road:
Being able to see all the fans in all the amazing cities every day

Worst part of being on the road:
Late nights, early mornings

Favourite place in the world:
America

Favourite video game:
Mario Kart Wii

Favourite thing to do as a family:
BBQ

JOE

My name is Joseph Adam Jonas, and I was born on 15 August 1989. I am one of the lead singers, and I play the tambourine, percussion, keyboard and a little guitar. I am the middle brother, two years younger than Kevin and three years older than Nick. I'm considered to be the 'funny' brother, and I always thought I'd end up in comedy . . . not music!

I'm definitely the guy that people assume is constantly bouncing off the walls. It's true that's me a lot of the time – I am definitely energetic. I love to be goofy and have a good time, but I also have a serious and more sensitive side that I don't always get to show onstage. A good friend once came to the studio while we were recording who seemed genuinely perplexed by my quiet demeanour. She said she expected me to be a lot livelier than I was and kept asking if something was wrong. I found myself explaining to her that I wasn't always the crazy guy she sees. Okay, ninety per cent of the time I am, but for whatever reason, that other ten per cent is a shocker!

My brothers often tell me that I have the biggest heart in the world. That makes me feel really good because I genuinely care about my family, friends and loved ones. I also care about the fans who come to see us. I want to make sure they have a good time, and I'm willing to do whatever it takes to make their experience unforgettable.

Top: Thumbs up!

Bottom: Just doing my thing.

Right: Cooling off after pouring water over my head and shaking it like a dog.

Trying to smile, even though we were running late for our show in Kansas City. I am the guy who makes it to the show just in the nick of time. If you ever come to one of our shows, I'm usually the last brother to go on stage.

Taking a few minutes to myself after a long flight to London. We were there for a photo shoot. Unfortunately, I was a little jet-lagged that day, but I was able to pull it together before the shoot.

Checking my phone for messages and trying to beat my own record on *BrickBreaker*. I get so frustrated when playing on the tour bus because one good bump makes my phone freeze up. So if I'm in the middle of a really good game, it messes everything up!

Left: This pretty much captures who I am. A fan gave me that sombrero during our show in Houston, Texas. Fan gifts are awesome! I was so happy to put it on and had so much fun wearing it while singing! *Olé!*

Right: It's a bird, it's a plane, it's Joe Jonas!

The Polaroids

Documenting our time on the road began to take on a whole new meaning when we bought a Polaroid camera that was for sale in our hotel before doing a show in Minneapolis. We started taking pictures right away and have basically never stopped since. I really became the keeper of the camera. Taking candid shots is something I love doing. I began archiving days, weeks and months on the road. Sometimes I took photos every single day, sometimes just occasionally. There's something about the rawness and imperfection of a Polaroid photo that feels so intimate and in the moment. The imagery is classic. Even though we have the best photographer in the business travelling with us to capture images, he's not with us 24/7. And, even if he is there, the quality of a perfectly shot digital photo and the quality of a Polaroid can't begin to compare. In this digital, 'Photoshop' world where everything is so perfect, revealing imperfections can be quite beautiful. I am certain these photos will become some of my favourite keepsakes years down the road. Looking back on them will remind me of how awesome these days were and how lucky we were to have them.

BEST ICE CREAM EVER

SKITTLES.

CAN'T LIVE

MIAMI, FL

HELICOPTER TO ALANTIC CITY

HISTORY.

FRANK J.

BRIDGE SWEET BAHAMAS!

DEER IN HEADLIGHTS

ST. LOUIS MUSEUM!

WE LOVE FANS

ROCKIN.

?

WHOEVER OWNED THIS CAR. SORTY I scratched it

SUMMER 07

SCARY BACKSTAGE

WRITING SESSION WITH DEMI. NICK ROCKIN

SAY WHAA?

CAN'T LIVE WITHOUT

OUR BAND OUR BEST FRIENDS.

WHAT I SEE.

MR. PRESIDENT

NICK J.   J. T.

ARIZONA

WHEN YOU CAN'T SEE THE BACK. ALL YOU CAN DO IS :)

BIG ROB PRODUCTIONS

ST. LOUIS. FAVORITE ICE CREAM

WE WILL DO THIS FOREVER...

I love this picture because it captures my passion for cinematography and film.

Below: I found this sailor hat in a costume shop. It must have been a cold day because I had a sweatshirt and a warm coat on. I don't usually bundle up unless it's really freezing.

Above: Shopping in London. The stores there are incredible. It's great to explore a city by walking around and checking out the local shops while searching for unique and different things that we can't necessarily find back home.

Style

I'll be the first to admit that I shop a lot. I pack my suitcase super light before we go on tour because I know I am going to fill it up along the way. I end up with too many clothes by the time we get home. My style is inspired by 1980s rock 'n' roll. I love wearing vintage band T-shirts, sneakers and straight-legged jeans. I really like shopping for shoes, but I don't like wearing socks, so most of my shoes are loafers or sneakers. I wear boat shoes as often as I can. I love to dress comfortably all the time and rock it up even when I'm not on stage.

If this move looks slightly familiar, it's because I am doing my karate kick that I learned from Koichi Sakamoto, a stuntman from the original Japanese Power Ranger series. He trains all of the current Power Rangers and also instructed my brothers and me in Kung Fu. I incorporated some of his teachings into my performance while singing 'Hold On'.

Musical Influences

I love Radiohead, Coldplay, a new band called the Neutrons, Johnny Cash, Elvis Costello, the Doors and the Rolling Stones. Mick Jagger is one of my heroes and has definitely influenced the way I perform.

I use the tambourine a lot. It's an instrument I love that I was inspired to learn by listening to the band Oasis, who use it often in their songs. You don't hear tambourine a lot these days, but I think it's cool to put it back in the spotlight.

Broadway vs. Jonas Brothers Performances

When I was younger, I had a role in the Broadway show *La Bohème*. Nick did several big shows on Broadway over the years, so I was very familiar with the routine and demands of doing eight performances a week. The biggest difference between doing a Broadway show and performing in the Jonas Brothers is that, in the band, we are really just being ourselves onstage. We get to sing songs we wrote out of our life experiences, which makes the music so much more personal.

Doing Broadway is the same performance eight times a week. There's not a lot of improvization or room to deviate from the script. When we are doing a Jonas Brothers show, we can change it as often as we'd like. Sometimes we add in a few new songs to test them out. We like to get the audience's reaction to our work in progress to see if they like the direction we're moving in. If we feel the audience didn't connect with the song, we know it's time to go back into the studio and work on it some more until we get it right.

Below: Mike 'The Commish' Meehan and me. I work out with him before every show. I am wearing a Penn State T-shirt because a lot of people who work with us went to Penn State and have a lot of pride for their school. It has kind of rubbed off on me.

Left: Working out before a show really gets my energy going and helps me get pumped before the concert.

Above: I have to stretch before every show. I try to lift my foot as close to my head as I can. Matt Petroff, AKA 'Colonel', our tour manager, helps me prepare by pulling my leg up as far as it can go so I don't get hurt while performing, especially when I have to do the splits onstage. Matt is an actual colonel, so he really knows how to put me through the paces.

Working Out

I love working out, especially while we're on the road. Staying fit is something that I try to focus on because being onstage all the time can really wear you down. I do a lot of cardio and weightlifting to help keep me in peak performance shape. I generally train with one of our security guys, who we call 'The Commish.' He's really ripped and in very good condition. I like to go running, so he usually goes with me and always pushes me to my limit.

My Favourite Things

Favourite ice cream:
Chocolate marshmallow

Favourite movie:
Four Feathers

If I could have lunch with anyone, dead or alive, it would be:
Abraham Lincoln

Favourite sport:
Soccer

Best day ever:
Playing the Texas State Fair

Definition of joy:
When you're happiest and nothing can change what you're thinking

If I weren't a pop star, I'd like to be:
Captain of a sailing ship

Something no one knows about me:
I'm a certified New Jersey babysitter

Favourite musician:
Paul McCartney

Most influential person(s) in my life:
My brothers and my Dad

Best advice someone gave me:
'Even if you're at the top, live like you're at the bottom.'
– Kevin Jonas (our Dad)

Favourite gadget:
My comb

I can't live without:
Air

Favourite place in the world:
Paris

Favourite thing to do as a family:
Sit around the dinner table and talk with one another

NICK

Hello, I'm Nicholas Jerry Jonas, and I was born on 16 September 1992. I also sing lead vocals, and play guitar, piano and the drums. Even though I am the youngest member of the band, I am considered to be the leader. I'm not really the 'boss', but I have a clear picture of who we are and where we're going. I am also considered the 'serious' one. I am independent, straightforward and yes . . . sometimes serious. When I'm not performing, I love to play golf, tennis and shoot some hoops. I've been told that I am extremely competitive, especially when it comes to sports. Being so driven has turned me into a fierce competitor. I am out to succeed in everything I do. That's just the way I roll.

If I weren't in the music business, I would love to spend more time in some of the amazing places I've seen. When I was done with that, I'd go to college. I always tell people that I'd like to run for president one day. If I did, I would definitely need a college degree for that! My nickname is 'The President'. I got it from being so determined all the time and for wanting to wear a suit.

At the end of the day, I am really just a nerd. I'm a music geek, the guy who would have been proud to be in the school choir or band. Music is a part of my DNA. From as far back as I can remember, I always knew it was my calling. I realize I'm living every kid's dream, and I am truly grateful for the opportunity.

Left: Playing 'Just Friends'. . . there are moments in every song where I love to rock out, and this is one of them.

Above: Doing my best Sherlock Holmes. This photo shows the elusive humorous side of me. Although it is rare, it does exist.

Right: I really like connecting with the audience during the show. I lock eyes with someone and play directly to them. It's great to make eye contact with a fan because it helps make the experience more intimate.

Style

I'm very frugal with my money, but I will spend it on certain must-haves. I have a weakness for ties, watches and nice shoes. I especially love classic ties by Ralph Lauren and Marc Jacobs, and love John Lobb shoes. One of my favourite sayings is: 'A tie makes the outfit and shoes make the man.' I try not to purchase things that feel unnecessary or superfluous. Being wasteful is not really my thing.

Above: Joe and I are checking our ties in the bathroom backstage before our show in San Antonio, making sure everything looks perfect.

Diabetes*

I was diagnosed with type 1 diabetes in November 2005 when I was thirteen years old. My diagnosis happened during the early days of our career. We had been touring schools all over the country, playing shows at 8:00 in the morning for kids in middle and high school. They'd look at us like we were crazy, because they had absolutely no idea who we were or why we were playing music at their school. It was a tough experience but one that taught us a lot about dealing with crowds.

About halfway through the tour, I noticed I was losing a lot of weight, drinking excessive amounts of water and frequently going to the bathroom. My parents began to notice a change in my attitude, too. I was unusually grouchy all the time. We didn't know it, but these were all symptoms of diabetes. Thinking I was just burned out, we took a week off from the tour and went on a family vacation.

When we came back I went to see our family physician to find out what was going on. After running several tests, she discovered my blood sugar level was off the charts. It was above 700, when a normal range is 70–120. As far as we knew, diabetes didn't run in our family, so it was a surprising diagnosis. I wasn't sure if this meant I could die. When I asked the doctor, she said I would be all right as long as I learned to monitor my blood sugar levels and watch the way I ate. Thankfully, I had my family all around me, so I wasn't going through this alone. It was a tough time that we got through together.

I spent a couple of days in the hospital so my blood sugar could be monitored and levelled out and so I could learn how to manage my diabetes. I had to learn how to count carbohydrates and watch my blood sugar, which I check twelve times a day. When I was released, I was feeling great – better than I had felt in a long time. We played a show the very next day. I promised myself that I wouldn't let the disease slow me down. I didn't want to let diabetes control me – I would control it. I knew I didn't have the time to be freaked out about the disease. I just had to do whatever it took to make it better before it got worse.

I wrote a song about diabetes called 'A Little Bit Longer'. I was in Canada shooting *Camp Rock,* and I was having one of those days where my blood sugar was a little bit out of control. I walked into a banquet room at the hotel where we were staying and saw a baby grand piano. Nobody was in there, so I sat down and began to play. Fifteen minutes later I called everybody into the room to come listen to the song. They all loved it. It was a really great feeling, because I had been feeling so down.

*For more information on diabetes, please go to:
nickssimplewins.org and *changeforthechildren.org*

A Little Bit Longer

Got the news today
But they said I had to stay
A little bit longer
And I'll be fine
When I thought it'd all been mine
When I thought it's all been said
A little bit longer
And I'll be fine

CHORUS
But you don't know what you got
Till it's gone
And you don't know what it's like
To feel so low
Every time you smile or laugh
You glow
You don't even know
No no
You don't even know

All this time goes by
Still no reason why
A little bit longer
And I'll be fine
Waiting on a cure
But none of them are sure
A little bit longer and I'll be fine
But you don't know what you got
Till it's gone
And you don't know what it's like
To feel so low
And every time you smile or laugh
You glow
No no
You don't even know

CHORUS

Two, three, four!

Yeah!
And you don't know what you got
Till it's gone
And you don't know what it's like
To feel so low
And every time you smile or laugh
You glow
You don't even know
No
Yeah
Whoa!

(oooohhhh)
So I wait till kingdom come
All the highs and lows are gone
A little bit longer
And I'll be fine
I'll be fine

The first time I played 'A Little Bit Longer' live
was at the Knitting Factory in LA after our show
at the Staples Center. The crowd went crazy.

Musical Influences

I love Elvis Costello, Johnny Cash and Prince. You can't get a wider mix than that. When I listen to their music, I feel something special. Even if I can't personally relate to the words in their songs, I know they were meaningful to these artists. It's really cool to listen to someone else's music and allow it to inspire your own writing. I like to take the funk feel of Prince's music and add some Johnny Cash storytelling with a touch of Elvis Costello rhythm behind it when I am writing songs.

A lot of people don't know that I've been playing drums longer than guitar. I started on bongos when I was very young – about five – and taught myself how to play. I've learned a lot by watching other great musicians over the years. We keep two sets of drums onstage during our shows, so Jack Lawless, our drummer, and I can both play.

My Favourite Things

Favourite ice cream:
Cotton Candy from Dairy Queen

Favourite movie:
Juno

If I could have lunch with anyone in the world it would be:
Elvis Costello

Definition of joy:
Music

Best day ever:
Denver, Colorado, the day we played trampoline dodgeball and rode go-karts

Favourite sport:
Baseball

Most influential person in my life:
My father

Favourite gadget:
My BlackBerry

I can't live without:
Insulin

If I weren't a pop star, I'd like to be:
A professional golfer

Worst part of being on the road:
Waking up really early. The best gift anyone can give me on the road is two extra hours of sleep!

Favourite place in the world:
Chicago

Favourite musician:
Stevie Wonder

Favourite thing to do as a family:
Eat a nice dinner together

FRANKIE

Hi! I'm Franklin Nathaniel Jonas and I was born on 28 September 2000. Most people call me Frankie, but I'm also known as the Bonus Jonas. I'm pretty good with music, just like my brothers. I'm already writing songs and I love to play the drums! I even have my own band. I like going on the road with my brothers, mostly to beat them at video games.

Below: Introducing Frankie to the audience for the first time in Boston. How cool is our little brother, rockin' a Ramones T-shirt and knit hat? He's the man!

Above: You can tell Frankie is riding his scooter pretty fast by how blurry the image of the person in the background is. He is fearless and fierce.

Left: Frankie's banging away on the drums during rehearsal for the upcoming tour.

Texas State Fair

We heard there were going to be a lot of people at the Texas State Fair, but we had no idea just how many of our fans would be there to greet us. It was unbearably hot outside – the temperature reaching 97 degrees around showtime, with the humidity at a brutal 42 per cent. Someone told us that people had actually started lining up around two o'clock in the morning so they'd be close to the stage.

Getting to the fairgrounds became a real challenge for us because the traffic was tied up for miles. There was no way we'd make it on time if we drove, so we ended up taking a helicopter. Flying in was amazing! We flew over the line of cars that dotted the road leading to the venue. As we got closer, we could see thousands of people from the air, but we still had no idea just how many there were. The whole scene felt like a true rock-star moment for us. We were definitely getting all hyped up.

When we got there, we had some time to visit our good friend Demi Lovato, who we had filmed *Camp Rock* with. After spending two months together making the movie, we got to know each other pretty well. It had been only a couple of weeks since filming wrapped, but it felt like much longer. We love when our friends can stop by and visit because we don't get a chance to keep up like we used to before we started touring. It was awesome to see Demi, but soon enough we had to say goodbye because it was showtime.

We finally caught a glimpse of the huge crowd as our bodyguard, Big Rob, walked us to the stage. We were blown away when we realized there were 50,000 people there! At the time, that was the largest live audience we'd ever played to. We couldn't believe what we were seeing. It freaked us out, but in a good way. We were totally pumped to go out there and give it our all.

The extreme heat didn't stop us from putting on one of our best shows ever. The crowd was all squished together, rocking along with us. We later heard that two hundred kids were treated for heat exhaustion. Thankfully, no one had to be sent to the hospital. This was definitely one of our all-time favourite shows. Everyone had a good time, which is what we always strive for!

59

American Music Awards

It was a huge thrill for us when we were asked to perform at the 2007 American Music Awards! It was our first time on a big awards show. We weren't nominated for anything, so it was an even greater honour just being asked to perform. We wanted everything to be perfect, since we knew that for many, this would be the first time they saw or heard the Jonas Brothers.

We didn't know what to expect. We had to go out there and give it our all. While we rehearsed, we were reading all the big celebrity names that were taped to the empty seats in front of us. It was cool to think we'd soon be performing in front of all of these talented artists.

We choreographed a really cool opening for our song 'S.O.S.' where we were supposed to appear onstage by crashing through special plate glass that was designed to shatter on impact. Once we cleared the broken glass, the song would start. Unfortunately, things don't always go as planned. Although everything was perfect during our rehearsal, the actual show would bring a total surprise . . .

As the time for our performance quickly approached, we stood backstage psyching ourselves up. We were totally focused on going out there to rock. The stage director told us to take our spots behind the glass. We were ready, and everything seemed perfect. We walked through the glass and then, as Joe was stepping through his glass, he accidentally tripped and fell in front of millions of viewers and a live audience full of music's biggest and best. There was a sudden gasp from the audience, because the tumble looked pretty bad. Joe jumped to his feet as if nothing had happened, and we began to play.

When we finished the song, we got backstage and realized Joe was hurt. Blood was all over his white suit, but he wasn't going to let that moment define him as a performer or take away from having the honour of being asked to play at the American Music Awards. In the end, it was an incredible experience, one we'll never forget.

I'm not really sure where my courage came from, but I wasn't about to let a little slip ruin our night. I jumped to my feet as fast as I could. In my mind, I started thinking about the possible reactions I could have had. Getting up and walking off the stage wasn't an option. I didn't want to look back on this experience with any regret, so I knew I just had to get up and perform with all my heart. Even though I had cut myself badly, I didn't feel any pain. I took all of that adrenaline rushing through my body and made it work for me. I ended up giving one of the best performances of my life.

PORTLAND

JONAS BROTHERS
WED FEB 6
7PM

Snapshots from the Road

Want to know what life on the road is really like? We have to admit . . . it's pretty cool. Even though it's a great adventure, it can also be very hectic a lot of the time! Our days are jammed from the moment we wake up until our heads hit the pillow at night. It can start as early as 4 a.m., when we might have to do interviews for various newspapers, magazines or news channels. And then we might be off to do a radio show for a couple of hours. By 3:00 in the afternoon, it's time for our sound check to make sure everything is perfect for the show later that night. We squeeze in our meals whenever we can, to make sure we're well fed and ready to rock!

By the end of our show, we're tired, but our day doesn't end there. Depending on where we're at, we might have more press to do before we can finally call it a night. We feel so lucky and blessed, and definitely wouldn't change a thing! We've learned to soak in every experience we have, so we can learn as much as possible from all of it.

People often wonder if we ever get bored. Honestly, the answer is an emphatic 'No!' When you look at these photos, you can see that we're genuinely excited. Performing is a thrilling experience for us, and we truly love what we do.

THE RAVE
EAGLES BALLROOM

THE JONAS BROTHERS
DEC 7 103.7 KISS FM PRESENTS

SOLD OUT

PARK HERE

AMBASSADOR HOTEL

The best part of being on the road for me is seeing the fans and brand-new places and faces every single day. On top of that, I get to do it while playing our music. What could be better than that?

– Kevin

My favourite thing about being on the road is the opportunity to travel and sightsee all over the world. I also really enjoy getting to meet our fans every place we go. It's fun to talk with people who speak all different languages. I always make it a point to thank them for coming out and supporting our music. That's one of the best parts of my job.

– Joe

The thing I like most about being on tour is being able to play a show every night. For me, that's one of the most amazing things in the world because I get to live my dream. When I was around six or seven years old, I used to make stages in the basement of our home and put on shows. I was certain that I would someday grow up and become a performer. As long as I can remember, that's all I've ever wanted to be. These days, I still have a passion for creating a stage, only now, they're much bigger and far more elaborate than the ones I built in my childhood.

I have a big part in everything that goes into creating our shows. I guess I learned about creative control very early on and have never given up since.

– Nick

Left: For the Mall of America show, we had to get up at the crack of dawn. We slept all night on the bus. Joe is making a bowl of cereal while Kevin is checking his e-mail. Our drummer, Jack Lawless, also known as 'Flawless Lawless', is hanging out with us too. This is a pretty typical morning on the bus.

Below: We had to get up really early for an appearance on *Good Morning America*. I was totally wiped out, struggling to keep my eyes open, but was also really excited because of the crowd that had come to see us that morning. If they could get up early and be there for us, I was ready to get out there and give my all for them.

The long days are hard but worth every minute. I've learned to soak up each experience we're having, good and bad, and learn from it. Since I'm not in college right now, I look at our travels as the best education I could be having.

– Kevin

The hardest part of being on the road for me is the lack of sleep. The early mornings are tough. I always find myself lying in bed wishing I had two more hours!

– Nick

I sometimes miss my own bed, pillows and Mom's home cooking, but there's not too much for me to genuinely complain about. I don't get that tired on the road because I really just enjoy being out there and having fun.

– Joe

A difficult aspect of touring is that we really miss our friends and family who aren't able to travel with us. We do our best to keep in touch but it can be a challenge when we're travelling in different time zones, sometimes with a six- to nine-hour time difference. Good friends are hard to come by, so when you know who your real friends are, it's important to keep in touch, even when you're super busy.

We try to meet up with friends from home when we're on the road, whether they live in the city we're visiting or fly in to wherever we are to join us for a couple of days. It's fun for them to see what it's like to be on tour and even sleep on our tour bus with us. It's the best thing in the world because they get to experience something brand new with us. We're all discovering something together at the same time. It could be a new city, a great museum or an amazing restaurant. It doesn't matter what we're doing as long as we're with people we love.

Recently we've met many people who are also in the business, so they really understand the demands and pressures we face. It's nice to have that kind of connection, because we can relate to each other in ways some of our friends who aren't in the industry can't understand. Since we aren't going to a traditional school or working nine-to-five jobs, having friends who do the same type of work as we do gives us someone to talk to about business-related stuff that we're going through. Sometimes they'll have insight and experience that help us navigate our own way.

In Our Spare Time . . .

When we aren't performing, we often have other events, such as parades, personal appearances and talk shows. Since we're on tour all the time, we tend to do these types of things during the day in the various cities where we're already there to play. We really like the opportunity to meet our fans up close and to play a few songs for them along the way.

Left: Doing a morning promo at a Long Island radio station. It was getting close to Christmas, which meant we'd get a little time off for the holidays. The tie Nick is wearing is one of his favorites. It's green-and-blue striped – totally classic.

Below: Trying to wake up during a very early morning interview at Radio Disney. Kevin and Nick drink coffee, but Joe doesn't. He definitely needed a boost that morning. Unfortunately, orange juice wasn't enough to get him going.

Macy's Thanksgiving Day Parade

This was our second year doing the Macy's Thanksgiving Day Parade. It was awesome and a real honour to be included. It was the first time the producers had a band participate two years in a row. Doing the parade definitely helps get me ready for the holidays.

I love being with my family to celebrate Christmas. I truly enjoy getting into the holiday spirit by just being together and giving gifts. Christmas has always been very special in our home.

- Nick

New Year's Eve 2007

We finished out 2007 by performing on Dick Clark's annual *New Year's Rockin' Eve* television special in Times Square. Joe really dressed for the occasion, choosing to wear a bow tie and top hat – after all, there aren't a lot of occasions to wear either these days. The coat he was wearing was really heavy. It was inspired by fashions from the 1800s, and it totally kept him warm on that very cold winter night.

Left: This was our first time performing live at the *Jimmy Kimmel* show. We played the Pontiac stage outside his studio to a huge crowd and hundreds of other people who watched the show from the rooftops of surrounding buildings.

Right: Ellen DeGeneres surprised us when she broke the news on her show that our album had sold a million copies. We had no idea she would present us with our actual platinum albums!

Left: Enjoying an arcade in Boston for a *People* magazine photo shoot. I loved being in the arcade. I won a lot of tickets to cash in that day. I gave them to a little boy who was hanging out the whole time we were there. He was thrilled, and so was I when I saw the look on his face after I handed the stack over to him.

Left: Trying to figure out what that German teen magazine had written about us!

Right: Signing autographs for fans while in Germany. We were there doing a shoot for *Bravo* magazine, one of their biggest magazines.

Left: Doing interviews with the German press is always interesting. They like to ask crazy questions we can't really answer but that always make us laugh.

Right: Relaxing during a video shoot in Germany. Nick is actually smiling, which doesn't happen a lot on camera.

A Little Fun on the Side

People are curious about how we spend our time on the road when we aren't performing. We love the rare opportunities we get to take some time for ourselves, away from the media and the spotlight. They help reinvigorate us and give us those little breaks along the way so we can keep up our wild pace.

Our favourite way to relax is to find the nearest golf course. We *love* to play golf. All of us are huge golfers and look forward to spending our days off at whatever course we can find nearby.

Golf is really relaxing for us because we enjoy the peace and solitude away from our usually frantic world. Our Dad joins in on the fun, along with Josh, our tour manager, and anyone else who might want to play eighteen holes. Some of our best ideas for touring and songs come from being out on the course. We can actually let our thoughts wander for a few hours.

My Mom had just told me to put on my jacket because it was too cold outside. I didn't want to because we were in San Diego and I didn't think it was that cold, but I listened to Mom anyway. When it came time to take the official photo of me riding the Segway, I had to take the jacket off because I didn't want to be photographed in it.

– Joe

Sometimes we go bowling, play a baseball game in the parking lot of an arena or throw the football around just to blow off some steam. We sightsee or keep it simple and go see a movie. It doesn't matter what we do as long as we're having fun, laughing and enjoying each other's company.

After a long day we're usually pretty hungry. When we're travelling to foreign countries, we try to taste as many new dishes as we can. Sometimes we like them – other times, not so much. We loved the food in Italy, and the Spanish food in Barcelona was also delicious. But there's nothing as good to us as some old-fashioned New York-style plain cheese pizza or an all-American burger!

Another thing we love to do in our spare time is check out other bands. We try to go see groups perform as often as we can. It's one of the great benefits of being on tour. We get to enjoy other people's music, hear what they're doing differently, and take in all of the amazing talent in this world. It is really inspiring because it pushes us to be even more creative.

Discovering new music is one of the best things. Not only do we appreciate what we're hearing, it also helps us understand how our fans feel when they listen to our music.

Left: Just obeying the sign.

Below: The obligatory red phonebox photo, with Joe wearing a Manchester United scarf.

The White House

One of the highlights of the past couple of years was when we visited the White House. We got to go three separate times, including the Easter Egg Roll, the official T-Ball kickoff with President Bush and the Correspondents' dinner. The White House is a really cool place, and it was such an honour to be invited.

Above: Nick Jonas for President! Our family during a visit to Washington, D.C., in front of the White House.

THE PERFECT DAY OFF

BY NICK JONAS

One of the best days off I've ever had was when we got to play trampoline dodgeball and ride go-karts. We were in Denver, Colorado, filming our reality show called *Living the Dream*, when we drove by this place that had a huge banner in front that read TRAMPOLINE DODGEBALL HERE! None of us had ever heard of that, so we begged to stop and check it out. It looked really cool, but we couldn't play right then because we had to get to the venue for our show. The next day, however, we took our whole band and crew and went back to discover trampoline dodgeball. Here's how it works: trampoline jumpers are the ball throwers. They get on the trampoline and bounce up and down. All the other players are allowed to roam in a marked-off area about 10 feet away from the trampoline. The people on the trampoline can throw the ball at the players on the ground in the marked-off area. You can only throw the ball while you're in the air. Any player tagged with the ball is then out. The last person standing is the winner.

It was awesome.

From there we went go-karting, which was a lot of fun, too. It was the ideal one-two punch of a perfect day off.

Songwriting and Recording

We can write songs any time, any place. We've written on aeroplanes and in bathrooms, on the bus or in our hotel room. The showers in the venues where we play make the best sounds because they're so big. It doesn't matter where we are, as long as we're in a groove. We'll sometimes sit around and philosophize about life until a theme or idea hits us that seems like the direction we want to go in.

When everything is perfect, we can write and record a song in one day. The sound engineer plays back the track as we try to figure it out and lay in cool sounds that fit the tune. We record everything when we're in the studio to make sure we don't miss a thing. We'll later sit around and listen to what we recorded that day. We might love what we hear and leave the song alone, or we might get inspired to do something totally different. It's all part of the process. Sometimes we have to walk away from a song for a few days to let our heads clear. That usually gives us better ideas for the song whenever we come back to it.

I wrote our song 'S.O.S.' at home in New Jersey after a date that went terribly bad. I was a bit frustrated because I really liked the girl. I went home and wrote 'S.O.S.' in about fifteen minutes while sitting on the couch in our family room. I was going through my first real big heartbreak. Originally, it was a song for my ears only so I could get over the pain from the date gone awry and to release my emotions. I had a hunch there was something special about the song, so I first played it for Kevin, who immediately said he was convinced it could be a big hit. I then woke my Dad to play the song for him. Despite being a little groggy, he agreed with Kevin. Once we played it for our producer, John Fields, we all hoped it would be a smash. We lucked out because a year later 'S.O.S.' was all over the radio.

It was the craziest thing in the world to suddenly hear my innermost feelings being sung by people when I initially meant it to be so personal and private. I wasn't looking to write a hit song – I was trying to get over a heartache. Knowing that something good came out of my pain made it all worthwhile.

I want our fans to be able to relate to the things we're going through. We know that other kids our age go through the same pain and anguish. Music has such tremendous power to heal and bring people together. It's a privilege to write music that so many different people can embrace. It's a great equalizer that puts all of us on common ground.

Most of the songs I write are songs of inspiration. Since we're so close as brothers, we have a way of communicating through our music. It's our way of talking to each other and conveying how we're feeling at a particular moment in time.

We'll come up with some chords that we'll play around with and then begin to add layers of music and lyrics. Since our process tends to be more spur of the moment, we usually end up writing all of our lyrics on a computer or a cell phone or PDA. We type as we go. It's a really cool process because it flows so naturally from each of us. Writing songs is definitely one of our biggest passions, and it's a great outlet.

We are truly collaborative in everything we do. Our success is very much a group effort. It may come as a surprise that we actually prefer it that way. We never focus on who started writing a particular song because once it's a song, it belongs to all of us. We are in this together from beginning to end – like the Three Musketeers, we're all for one and one for all.

S.O.S.

I told you I made dinner plans
For you and me and no one else
That don't include your crazy friends
Well I'm done with awkward situations
Empty conversations

CHORUS
Oooo, this is an S.O.S.
Don't wanna second guess
This is the bottom line
It's true
I gave my all for you
Now my heart's in two
And I can't find the other half
It's like I'm walkin' on broken glass
Better believe I bled
It's a call I'll never get

So this is where the story ends
A conversation on IM
Well I'm done with texting
Sorry for the miscommunication

CHORUS

Next time I see you
I'm giving you a high five
'Cause hugs are overrated
Just FYI

CHORUS

I am extremely proud of all of our songs, but 'Goodnight and Goodbye', 'S.O.S.' and 'Lovebug', from *A Little Bit Longer,* are three of my favourites.

In my opinion, 'Lovebug' is probably the best song we've recorded to date. It's different from a lot of the other ones we've written. It's about that feeling you get when you fall in love after recovering from a breakup. Just when you thought you'd never have those feelings again, along comes someone who rocks your world. We wrote 'Lovebug' over the course of four days we had off during the Best of Both Worlds tour.

We took a risk with it by incorporating all sorts of devices that were unusual choices for us, such as talking and using unique musical instruments, especially crazy percussion. We had a vision of how that song sounded in our heads and recorded it exactly that way. The idea was to sound as though we were performing the song in a crowded coffee shop where no one is paying attention to what we're singing about. We keep playing, trying to get their attention, until we realize we just have to rock it out. That's pretty much how we approached recording the song. It's a slow build to a really heavy ending.

– Nick

Left: This keyboard has a built-in microphone that records your voice in the same key you're playing in. We liked to say a lot of funny things into it. We'd play it back and crack up at how hilarious we sounded. I was just goofing around this time, but I hope to use it someday to write a song.

Above: Recording 'Sorry' for the new album. The song is sort of an apology for breaking promises I wasn't around to keep. It's about being on the road and far away from someone.

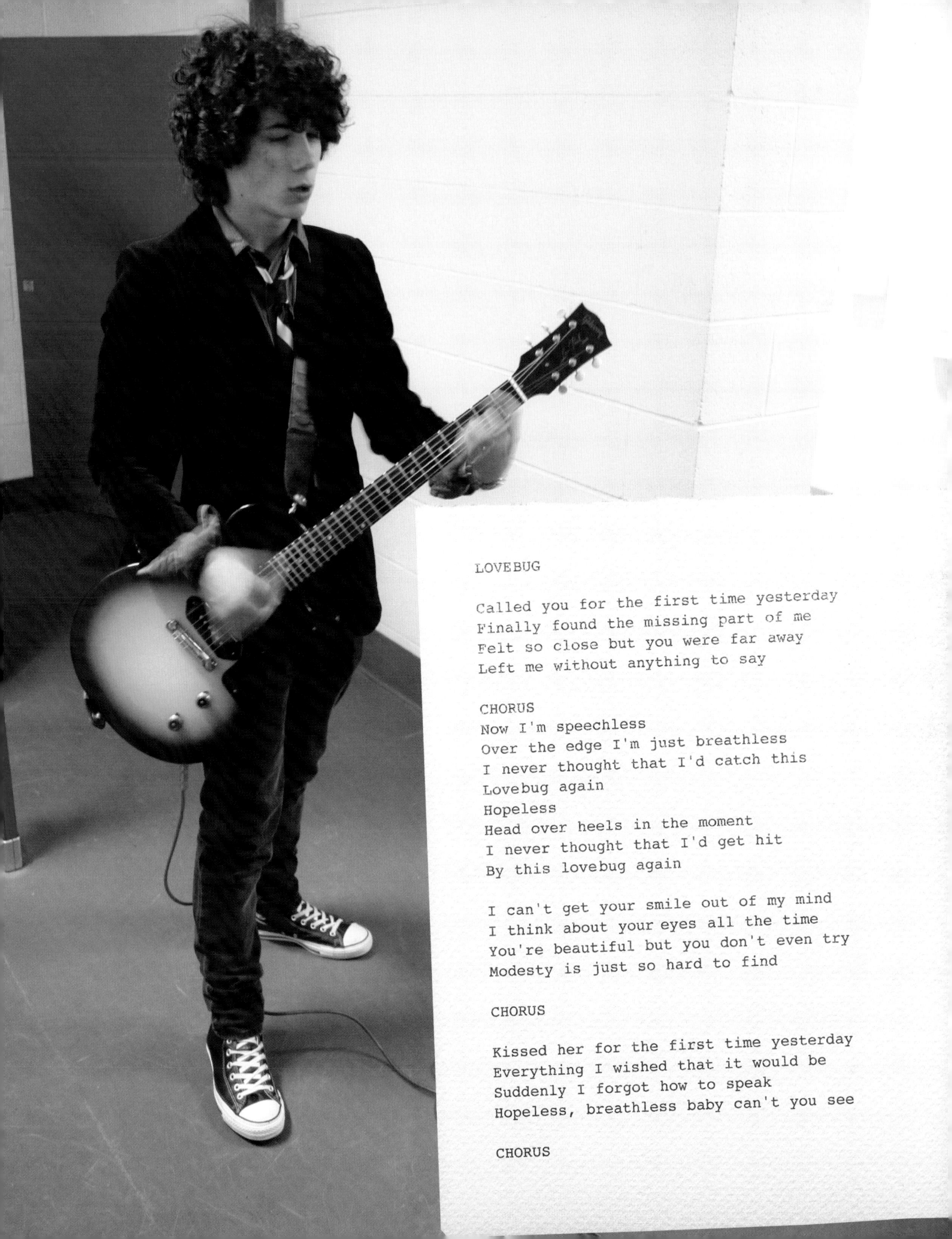

LOVEBUG

Called you for the first time yesterday
Finally found the missing part of me
Felt so close but you were far away
Left me without anything to say

CHORUS
Now I'm speechless
Over the edge I'm just breathless
I never thought that I'd catch this
Lovebug again
Hopeless
Head over heels in the moment
I never thought that I'd get hit
By this lovebug again

I can't get your smile out of my mind
I think about your eyes all the time
You're beautiful but you don't even try
Modesty is just so hard to find

CHORUS

Kissed her for the first time yesterday
Everything I wished that it would be
Suddenly I forgot how to speak
Hopeless, breathless baby can't you see

CHORUS

While touring, we found time to record our album *A Little Bit Longer*. We did most of the recording on the Gibson Tour Bus, which was completely fitted out with the most up-to-date studio on wheels we've ever seen. We had all the equipment we needed, and John Fields, our producer extraordinaire, was there every step of the way. The bus was on the road with us the entire Best of Both Worlds tour, so all of our spare time was dedicated to writing and recording. When we weren't playing shows, we were recording.

Right: Talking about the new album at Wishbone Studios in L.A. with John Fields. We were working on 'Sorry', a song we wrote with John.

There's a song on *A Little Bit Longer* called 'Can't Have You' that came from one of our group sessions. It's all raw emotion and pure intentions. It's about not letting your life go by and disappear without a moment's notice. If I'm in love, I am not going to let her go. I'm going to fight for her until the day I die. For me, that is just the way I do things. And the same philosophy holds true for our music. I'll fight to write music we love and to play music we are passionate about. You have to fight for everything you believe in or it will inevitably disappear.

CAN'T HAVE YOU

Warned me that you were gonna leave
Never thought you would really go
I was blind but baby now I see
Broke your heart now I know
That I was being such a fool
And I didn't deserve you

CHORUS
Don't want to fall asleep 'cause I don't
know if I'll get up
Don't want to cause a scene but I'm dying
without your love
Begging to hear your voice
Tell me you love me too
'Cause I'd rather just be alone
If I know that I can't have you

Lookin' at the letter that you left
Wondering if I'll ever get you back
Dreaming about when I'll see you next
Knowing that I never will forget
That I was being such a fool
And I still don't deserve you

CHORUS

Well tell me what we're fighting for
'Cause we know that the truth means so
much more
'Cause you would if you could don't lie
Well I'll give everything that I've got
left
To show you I mean what I have said
I know I was such a fool
But I can't live without you

CHORUS x2

Rockin' Out

Performing is part of us. We wouldn't know how to function without our music. If we weren't playing together, our relationships might not be as close as they are. We'd probably have more typical brother-to-brother relationships because we'd be living independently of one another. But since we play in a band, there's a different mind-set and a higher respect for each other. It's hard to describe because being together as a group is all we really know. Performing is the thing we love most. It's everything we've worked towards and all that we want to do. It's incredible to be onstage, hear our fans sing along with us and have a good time doing it.

Above: That's Nick doing an aerial, a no-handed cartwheel, down a ramp during the Best of Both Worlds tour. He always likes bringing some theatrics to the stage during our shows. He loved doing this move so much that he incorporated it into the Look Me in the Eyes and Burning Up tours.

t: This move is so much fun – Joe pulls k over his shoulder using one hand while h of them keep singing. *Rock 'n' roll!*

I hope I never get tired of performing. I am certainly not planning on it, but if I do, I will have to figure things out when I get there. There's always something brand new coming round the corner. Who would have guessed we'd be writing a book or starring in movies? It's amazing how fast things can happen in life. In the meantime, I get to be onstage, playing guitar and doing what I am most passionate about every day.

– *Kevin*

Below: Joe knocked his keyboard off its stand because he was so excited to celebrate the last performance of the Best of Both Worlds tour. He later found out he had to buy it because he'd broken it. That was an expensive lesson that taught him never to do that again!

The Knitting Factory

We played the Knitting Factory in Los Angeles after our show at the Staples Center. The Knitting Factory is one of those venues that has launched careers and where bands come to do small, intimate shows. It's part of rock 'n' roll history. We took in the whole night as another new and incredible experience. Singers and songwriters we respect and admire had stood in the same room years before we ever did. Now we were inside. It was pretty amazing.

Super Secret Shows

From time to time we like to do what we call Super Secret Shows. We've only done a few, but they're always really exciting for us because we can play to a smaller audience, usually in a more intimate place.

We played one of our rare Super Secret Shows in late December 2007 while we were in Boston. It wasn't planned, but it was really fun. Twelve hundred fans who couldn't get into the earlier show listened to us jam with our full band. Being close to our fans is really important to us. Intimate shows used to mean the shows we played early on in our career when ten or so people would show up to hear us play, including the six members of the other band on the marquee that night. Those shows were kind of a bummer, but they made us so thankful for the smaller shows we get to play today.

Milwaukee, Wisconsin

While we were on the Best of Both Worlds tour, we broke away to do our own show in Milwaukee, Wisconsin. We didn't know what to expect because it was in a smaller venue than we had been playing the past few months with Miley Cyrus. The show was at the Eagles Ballroom, a historic club that was originally built in 1926. It had no seats, so the concert would be standing room only. Thirty-five hundred fans showed up for our show and had to crunch together so everyone could be a part of our very special night. This was one of our all-time favourite concerts ever because everything about it went right. It was a virtually perfect show – something we can't say very often.

We were in the midst of shooting a music video for 'When You Look Me in the Eyes', so a production crew was going to be filming the concert that night. The fans went wild when we took the stage, which surprised us since we hadn't anticipated such a large or enthusiastic crowd. By the end of the show, we were all exhausted yet so exhilarated by the experience we'd had.

Right: Our manager, Phil McIntyre, hanging out backstage at the Eagles Ballroom before our show. This is a glimpse of the downside of life on the road. His wife was back in California, and we were both pondering how much we missed our loved ones who couldn't be with us.

Backstage Pass

We know a lot of you would love the chance to come backstage to see what happens before and after one of our shows. We wish it was possible to meet each and every one of you, but since it isn't, here's an exclusive inside peek at what it's really like backstage through some of our favourite photos.

Left: This photo was taken right before we went onstage in San Antonio. Sometimes before a show I'll find myself playing a few chords that may (or may not) become a song later on. It's one of the ways I prepare and focus before going onstage.

Lockdown

Before every show we have a 45-minute lockdown where no one is allowed into the dressing room except us. We practise, warm up our voices, stretch and mentally prepare for the show. We allow people back about five minutes before we go onstage, when we gather in a circle and pray. At the end of our prayer, we place our hands together in the middle and say, 'Living the dream! Living the dream!' as a way to get ourselves psyched.

We don't believe in any superstitions about going onstage – we just have a routine. We give each other encouragement and always make sure to say we love each other and then go out there and do what we love to do most. We're like fighters getting pumped up before going into the ring for a championship bout. By the time we set foot onstage, we're ready to go a full fifteen rounds.

Left: Backstage with my Dad after our second set on the Best of Both Worlds tour. Dad always gives us updates in between sets – usually delivering good news that developed during the day. It's often career related, so it's encouraging as we get ready to head back onstage to take our bows.

Our Fans Rock!

Sometimes our fans can be, well, fanatical! It's a crazy feeling to find ourselves being chased by a group of people trying to get our autographs or take a picture with us. A few times our tour bus was followed by a caravan of cars, swerving and honking their horns, trying to get our attention. We hear them all night long, even when we're sleeping! We've kind of got used to it, but not so used to it that we aren't grateful for their tremendous enthusiasm.

It's kind of weird to think that when we were growing up our friends had posters of N*Sync and the Backstreet Boys on their walls and now people have posters of us. We know there'll be another band that comes along someday whose posters will replace ours, but until then we want to enjoy every moment.

Our fans play one of the biggest parts in how a performance turns out. We are totally committed to putting on the best show we can, but having the crowd's involvement can make the difference between a good show and a great show. The goal is to get everyone smiling and pumped. It's really nice to have the audience's energy to feed off. As a band, we fuel off one another, so that type of connection is in our roots. When the fans are excited, it really helps us get psyched and inspires us to give every ounce of energy until we literally have none left.

Above: People were actually trying to climb over the barbed-wire fence during a radio concert in Fresno, California. We didn't want anyone to get hurt, so Kevin sang a little while he signed autographs and Nick advised the crowd to be careful.

Left: This scrapbook is from a fan who filled it with one hundred reasons why she loves the Jonas Brothers. Gifts like this really inspire us to go out and have our greatest shows.

Some of our favourite concerts were the ones where there were tons of people who were just losing themselves in the music. Seeing thousands of screaming fans AND the looks on their faces will never grow old to us. We are so thankful for it. When we meet fans who tell us they were at one of our 'really awesome' concerts, we know what it meant to them because it was equally memorable for us. Those are moments we'll never forget.

Above and left: Verizon sponsored the fan promotional bus during the Look Me in the Eyes tour. The graffiti started when one fan left her phone number on the side. Once she did that, everyone jumped on the idea and began leaving messages for us. We didn't see the bus until the last day of the tour. When we finally caught a glimpse, our first reaction was 'No way!' There was spray paint on everything and people had used every inch of space to show us how much they care. This is probably the ultimate fan gift we've ever received.

This is what we refer to as 'fandemonium'! Fans were running after our car as we left an in-store appearance. We had to leave with a full police escort to make sure no one got hurt. Our photographer, Rob Hoffman, took this shot hanging out the back window of our car.

Atlantic City, New Jersey

While we were in Atlantic City to do a show, we met with a magazine writer and photographer. Even though it was a chilly winter day, the writer thought it might be really nice to get outside and take a stroll along the famous boardwalk so the photographer could grab a few candid shots. When we stepped outside, thousands of screaming girls came running toward us, seemingly out of the blue. Luckily, we were close to the entrance to Boardwalk Hall, where we were scheduled to play later that night. We escaped into the venue before things got too insane.

Left: About to leave the venue in Atlantic City while holding on to Big Rob so we can make it through the waiting crowds. People have no problem getting out of *his* way!

123

Our Family, Our Foundation

Our family is the single most important thing in our lives. While performing is what we do, family is the foundation for everything. Lucky for us, we all have a very open relationship with one another. Our Mom and Dad have made it easy for us to talk about things without feeling judged or afraid. Beyond their love and understanding, we have each other. We talk about all of the stuff that is going on in our heads, our lives and hearts. It's amazing to have that type of love and bond between us.

We really enjoy celebrating our lives' blessings. We always try to do something fun and spontaneous for each other's birthdays. Last year we celebrated Joe's birthday (which happens to be the same day as our parents' anniversary) by bringing a cake onstage at the end of our show. Kevin held the cake up so Joe and our parents could blow out the candles. Something happened, and before we knew it, the cake slid out of Kevin's hands and fell all over our Dad! We all laughed. Those are the times we will remember and cherish for the rest of our lives.

People sometimes wonder if we ever get into arguments or fights. It's true that most brothers will bicker from time to time, and we sometimes do, but we genuinely have love and total respect for each other. We can't really relate to someone who says they hate their brother or sister, and we're always surprised by that type of emotion because we really get along. We know we can't go onstage with a bad attitude, which means we can't be fighting with one another before a show. Perhaps if we were just a couple of guys in a band, things might be different. But we are three brothers who are in a band together, which makes it a lot easier to say 'I'm sorry' and talk things out.

We grew up together and know each other so well. Even if we stopped playing in a group, we are connected for the rest of our lives, so it makes sense to keep things cool. Besides, we enjoy what we do too much to risk losing a single moment of our blessings. If we look at things with that positive attitude, then it makes whatever the petty issue is seem so small and insignificant. In the scheme of life, we've got no complaints. If anything, we have so much to be grateful for.

I am a lot like my father. Our personalities are very similar in that we both are extremely dedicated, goal oriented and very driven. So it was just a natural progression for me to take a leadership role in the group. My brothers are really amazing guys to give me the respect of being their equal, even though I am younger than them. I've always had this passion to succeed. And because of the synchronicity between us as brothers, each of us has our place in the band, which helps us work off each other and not against one another.

Kevin is brilliant when it comes to the production. He is really good at figuring out all of the elements that will work for our live shows. He loves being a part of every last detail, especially when it comes to staging and effects. He's got a passion for the business side of things that seeps into everything we do.

Joe is the most awesome front man a band could ever have. He really knows how to control the crowd and all our fans. He's got an inherent talent – it's not something that can be learned. Fine tuned, perhaps, but it has got to be in your blood, your core, to really do what Joe does. And besides, he's so funny and knows how to lighten things up when needed. He makes us all laugh, and that's one of the best gifts he can bring to the group, especially when we are offstage and in need of some humour.

I've had a lot of dreams my whole life. One by one, I have been trying my hardest to accomplish each of them. My drive is a big part in making that happen. Without my father's influence, I wouldn't be where I am today.

– Nick

Above: This sign has one of our favourite Bible verses on it.

Right: That's our amazing friend Maya . . . she's the sister we never had. Maya's Dad and ours were best friends when our Dad was a minister in New Jersey. Maya's father became very ill several years ago and eventually passed away when Maya was nine months old. Our Dad promised him that he'd look after his family, and we've been inseparable ever since.

Right: The three of us hanging out in Germany.

Mom & Dad

Our parents have taught us everything we know. There's no telling where we'd be without their love, wisdom, guidance and support. They have remained hands-on throughout our career, but have never pushed us into doing anything we didn't truly want to do ourselves. They simply gave us the faith and strength to believe we could do anything we wanted because they unconditionally believe in what we're doing. They are right next to us in case we begin to drift, to remind us of how important it is to remain humble. We are so appreciative of their strength and faith in us – not as performers, but as a family.

It's really nice having our Mom and Dad on tour with us because it allows us to stay together as a family. It keeps us grounded and gives us a home base, even if we're thousands of miles away from 'home'. As long as we're together, we are home, regardless of where we are. We like having someone around to tell us we're doing a great job – even when we know we could be doing better. That's what parents do. Sometimes you just need your Mom to make sure you're taking care of yourself, eating right, getting enough sleep – and staying humble. Even when we're in a hotel, we crave Mom's cooking for comfort. She does her best to make sure we get whatever nourishment we need – whether it's food or love.

Top: Mom is probably telling me to clean up my bunk. The woman in the black-and-white striped shirt is Kyoko. She is Maya's Mom and our really good family friend.

Above left: Mom, Dad, and Frankie take a stroll.

Above right: Mom is the queen. The pillow was a Christmas gift to her from a friend.

Right: Mom and Maya

Mexico City, Mexico

After the excitement of playing to 50,000 fans at the Texas State Fair, we were shocked to find out we'd be facing 80,000 people when we played a festival concert in Mexico. This was our first experience with going to another country where the concertgoers were as enthusiastic as our American fans.

When we arrived at the stadium before the show, we couldn't get over how huge it was. We stood onstage trying to take everything in and comprehend the massive amounts of people that would soon fill the place just to hear us sing. It could have been really intimidating, but it wasn't. We always look at these opportunities as a chance to grow as performers.

Playing to a larger audience has its challenges. It's a lot harder to get 80,000 people to join in and sing along with us than it is a couple of thousand. If we're trying to get the crowd to move, wave or clap, our gestures have to be over-exaggerated so the people in the very back can join in on the fun too! Even the JumboTron screen looks far away in a stadium that big. But it's one of the most unbelievable feelings in the world to perform in front of such a huge group of people. We can feel the adrenaline pumping through our bodies as we step out onstage and hear the screaming fans. As the energy builds, we feel like we can do anything.

Top right: Before every show, Dad usually gives each of us some words of encouragement.

Bottom right: Whoa! We just realized what 80,000 people looks . . . and sounds like!

Our shows can be really emotional for us, but our performance in Mexico that night was something very special. We knew we had rocked it hard. The crowd was with us from the very first note, and after we sang our last song, we stood onstage for an extra moment just to absorb the energy and positive vibes that were coming our way like a huge tidal wave of emotion. We were relieved to be done and yet so thankful. Tears streamed down our cheeks with appreciation for all the love and adoration we received that night in Mexico.

East Rutherford, New Jersey

On the last night of our Look Me in the Eyes tour, we had the pleasure of playing the Izod Center – the largest arena near our hometown, Wyckoff, New Jersey. It was filled with family, friends and lots of fans. This show was one of the most meaningful we ever played because we were finally 'home'.

We used to go to the Izod Center as kids, and whenever we drove into Manhattan, we had to pass right by it. 'One day we'll play there,' we always said to each other. Now here we were – and not only were we about to play there, we had sold it out! It was incredible!

Above: Who says you can't go home again?

At the end of the show, we invited our family, friends, our opening band, Rooney, and crewmembers out onstage to help us sing 'We Are the Champions'. Everyone was crying because it was the end to such an awesome tour. We later celebrated the night with all of our closest friends and family at Planet Hollywood in New York City. It was a complete blast. All of us were so happy to have fulfilled our dream of playing that arena and a bit relieved that we had come to the end of our first headlining tour. Not only had we reached a monumental milestone in our career, but we also had found a sense of peace. We had truly achieved a moment in our career that could never be duplicated or repeated. That night in New Jersey was the end of our tour, but it was also the beginning of something amazing. It was the start of who we're going to be for years to come.

A Special Thank You...

We would like to thank our Lord and Saviour for blessing us with a dream come true.

Thank you to our family . . . Mom, Dad and Frankie. You are the foundation that makes every day possible. We love you and thank you so much.

To Coach and Maya . . . our two most loyal members on the road! You give us unconditional love and support and for that we are forever grateful to have you as part of our family.

A special thank you to our management team . . . Dad and Phil, you've taught us to believe in ourselves no matter what and to follow our hearts. We would not be where we are today without your guidance and leadership. Johnny Wright . . . thank you for instilling your wisdom in us every day. Thank you, Shonda McIntyre for letting Phil work so hard every day!

To Rob Brenner . . . We live the dream every day because of your tireless efforts. We know that our dreams become your problems and we appreciate it more than you know.

To our amazing tour crew . . . Thank you for working so unbelievably hard every day. We appreciate it very much.

To our band: Johnny T, Garbo, Jack and Ryan . . . You are our brothers and we thank you so much for being such a special part of this journey.

To the String Section . . . Our newest addition! You rock and we love having you as part of our family.

To Matt Petroff . . . You are our Colonel and we salute you.

To Big Rob . . . We are proud you walk ahead of us every day. Thank you for everything you do. YESSIR!

Fe . . . There is never a moment you are not there to take care of our every need and we thank you so very much.

To Mike Meehan . . . Thank you for your commitment to our family.

To Jennifer Webster, Erin Quandt and Jessica Andrews . . . Thank you for all your love and support every day.

To Ned Specktor . . . a warm welcome to our family.

To Bob Cavallo, Abbey Konowitch, David Agnew, Ken Bunt, Jon Lind, Stacy Satz, Lillian Matulic and everyone at Hollywood Records and Radio Disney; Live Nation; David Zedeck and Brian Manning and our team at CAA; Rob Cohen and our entire legal team at Carroll, Guido & Groffman; Glenn Nordlinger and the Nordlinger Group; Travel Like a Rockstar; Bruce Fingerett and everyone at FEA Merchandising; Sonia Muckle and everyone at M2M Construction; John McMahon and everyone at Change for the Children; Matt Ferguson and everyone at Gibson Guitars . . . Thank you all so much for your support and hard work. You each play such a critical role in our journey and we are lucky to have you in our lives.

A special thank you to Brad Wavra . . . Our biggest fan and backup dancer! Thank you for believing in us so much.

To Michelle Tomaszewski . . . You are such a special person and this book reflects the unique gift you share with the world.

To Rob Hoffman . . . A special congratulations on your first book! You should feel proud. Thank you for capturing our memories every day.

To Cat, Marissa and Amy . . . thank you so much for your patience and hard work.

To Jamma (Jeri DiSavino), Stella Psaroudakis, Kathy and Mandy VanDuyne, Dennis MacPherson, Joyce Kimberly Belitzsky, Kat and Bill Tilley, and all of the moderators . . . Thank you for dedicating so much time and effort to our fan club. It is such an important part of our lives and your contributions help make it what it is.

To the people who turned this project into a reality . . . Simon Green, Nancy Inteli, Stuart Smith, Jon Yaged, Wendy Lefkon, Rodger Weinfeld, Monica Mayper, Jessica Ward and Marybeth Tregarthen. Thank you for bringing this book to life.

To Bruce Kapp . . . We miss you very much and promise to make you proud every day.

To Steph, one of our original Street Teamers . . . life took you too soon, but it's comforting to know you are watching over us.

And most of all . . . Thank you . . . to our fans. You are the engine that drives us every day and your support means more than you'll ever know.

We love you.